This Is Why I Never Left

By: Milo Santamaria

DAXSON PUBLISHING

This is Why I Never Left
© 2025 Milo Santamaria
ISBN: 979-8-9900531-9-9
Library of Congress Control number: 9781966337126

Cover art:
© 2025, Milo Santamaria

© 2025, Interior Artwork, Milo Santamaria

First Edition, 2025

Printed in the United States of America

Edited by Milo Santamaria
Cover Design by Milo Santamaria
Layout Design by Erica Castro

For Shelly Leann West

"*In trying to get people to see your humanity, you reveal just that: your humanity. Your fundamentally problematic nature. All the unique and terrible ways in which people can, and do, fail.*"
- Carmen Maria Machado, In The Dream House

Table of Contents

Introduction

This Is Why I Never Left is a queer feminist poetry collection dedicated to ending cycles of abuse and violence. These poems reveal how abuse is not just a personal wound, it's also a cultural and political one.

This collection examines the stories we're told about relationships: the myths that teach us to settle for what harms us, to stay silent, to disappear. And it dares to imagine something different—what it might look like to build relationships rooted in safety, in wholeness, and the freedom to be fully ourselves without fear.

I started writing poems in community college. This book actually started as a silly journaling assignment for my queer literature class. I never really planned on publishing my writing but watching other girls go through similar experiences to me made me realize how important it was to have conversations about misogyny and abuse.

Because it took me years to realize that what I experienced at home as a child, and what I went through in relationships as an adult was abuse.

There were so many times that I wished I could speak up and stop what was happening to me, but somewhere along the way I started feeling powerless, and unable to prevent the violence and neglect I experienced, both at home and at school.

To cope, I got really good at dissociating, at watching my life from afar, pretending to not take things personally, at not being surprised when I was mistreated or ignored or neglected. I got good at taking up as little space as possible.

To avoid tripping over my words, sometimes I chose to stop speaking altogether.

The only time I felt really excited and like I had autonomy over my life is when I was finally getting ready to move to college as the world started to emerge from the covid-era-lockdowns. I spent 3 years in community college, taking all the right classes, and doing everything I needed to transfer to a university.

I saw college as an escape from my abusive house, from the comfortable Southern California environment I'd grown up in. So, I chose a university 300 miles away in the Redwood forest. Thinking an artsy coastal forest town was the one place I could finally be myself.

I had also avoided romantic relationships my whole life, knowing I was susceptible to some really unhealthy relationship dynamics because I'd been abused so much as a kid. But my ex was my friend, or at least I thought he was, and I was a silly college girl who wanted to fit in, have a boyfriend like all my friends had growing up. Thought I could handle a little college fling.

I saw the red flags, told myself "If anyone else was doing this I'd run," but he'd assure me he wanted me to feel safe, and I felt like graduation was my safe ticket out anyway, since he lived in the Bay Area, and I was always going to come back to Southern California after graduation. I never really wanted long distance.

I even flinched away when he tried to kiss me for the first time, something didn't feel right. We were alone in my room, and I was scared, but he almost started crying, "Ohhh...d-d-do you not like me?"

Honestly it had only been a month, I was still trying to get to know him and decide if this is what I wanted. And I knew everything was happening too fast, but my dissociation also kicked in quick, letting me believe the fantasy he sold me while my body tucked itself into its own dream to escape what was really happening.

Then I found out was talking to my "friend" the whole time, opening up to her instead of me, telling her god-knows-what about me, he even planned our breakup with her, and when he was too cowardly to go through with it, I had to do it. He made me the villain so he could cry to everyone about how I broke up with him.

Honestly this hurt me more than if he had been romantically into someone else, or physically cheated (though this could have happened too, I'll never know for sure) because all I wanted was to be emotionally close to him. I saw him more as a friend than a partner, it was always hard for me to see him that way, hard for me to want him that way.

Despite my experiences, and how much I've read about oppression and violence a younger more emotional part of me didn't want to believe the world was that bad, that people could be so cruel. I wanted to keep my little idealistic worldview even when I knew it was causing me harm. It's so much easier to think that there's something you can change about yourself to make the violence and abuse stop, than it is to acknowledge that there's no guarantee of safety in our current society.

I think the breakup finally tore through my illusions, and it was really painful, but I think I see the world more clearly now. My body feels also feels so much calmer now that it doesn't have to scream to get me to recognize danger.

And I also don't blame myself anymore, it took months of therapy, crying, and hanging out with my old high school friends to remember what safety felt like.

I had run away from home so much, I had run from my own emotions, I didn't even know what was real anymore, I couldn't tell the difference between the illusions I believed, and the stories I created to survive my pain. I needed to ground myself, I needed to come home, and choosing myself over my so-called-friends ended up being the key.

Back in SoCal it took me months to escape the fog in my head, it's like my body never left the forest, the flood of emotions and wounds I tried to run from came back, begging me to finally heal them, all the alarm bells in my body still ringing, long after the smoke had cleared.

But I told myself, if I was coming home to my body, I was going to make it the safe place I never had. The safe place I kept trying to find outside of myself. So, I healed years worth of trauma in the months after my breakup, all while juggling 2 internships and grad school courses. I was crashing out and trauma dumping all over my Instagram stories, but after a while I stopped caring about how people perceived me, I just needed to get it all out.

Then after a while, I noticed I didn't hate SoCal anymore. I got on the train I used to take to community college to meet my friends in Little Tokyo, looked out the window and remembered how pretty LA looks after the rain. I sat on a seaside cliff in San Diego, right after my last phone call with my ex, and realized that this wasn't a bad place to be heartbroken, I had the sea, and the mountains, and the citrus trees.

I started joining local activist communities, I volunteered at a community run bookstore, I picked vegetables at a community run farm, I took a poetry class, I connected with old friends and realized the whole time I'd been trying to escape my life, thinking I'd only be worth something if I moved away and got a degree...

I'd already been so loved by my friends, I'd accomplished so much, I lived in a beautiful city with people I appreciated, I realized my silly life had an impact on people, so I let go of the dream of running away, and finally started to feel deserving of my life.

What I've learned is that you can't earn your way out of experiencing systemic violence and oppression. Safety shouldn't just belong to those who have "earned" it, we all deserve to live in safe communities free from harm, regardless of how palatable we are to those in power.

My siblings and I grew up on this idea that we'd go to college, make it on our own and finally be free from our abusive childhood home. But I just ended up causing myself more pain and harm by pushing myself past my limits to earn degrees, and to prove I was worthy of being in academic spaces. I also made friends along the way that I really cared for, only to find that they hated me the whole time.

These oppressive systems where we feel forced to prove ourselves really impact our relationships and the ways we relate to each other. For example, girls often blame themselves for men's mistreatment like, "If I was prettier or more successful or different somehow this wouldn't happen to me."

I think that sometimes we forget that misogyny is a violent

form of oppression and things don't have to be physical to be violent or harmful or traumatizing. We're also taught to compete with other girls and that makes it so much harder to see that we're all experiencing the same issues and to identify the root cause. (though obviously all of us have different marginalized identities / privileged identities that impact how we experience misogyny and violence.)

Hearing other women's stories and advice on picking up red flags and staying safe has helped me feel less alone but sometimes I wish we didn't have to go through so much to keep ourselves safe. And I wish our desires for care and love and safety and pleasure were not constantly exploited by those in power.

This Is Why I Never Left was a way for me to discuss the harmful impacts of victim blaming and the shame that abuse survivors carry.

I've learned that what often determines whether you develop PTSD is the level of support you have in healing from the trauma. Part of the reason I think victim blaming is so damaging is because it disrupts the way your body heals itself.

When you don't feel supported or you're blamed for the mistreatment you endured, then you can end up with a lot of shame around your trauma responses. This often means you won't understand when your body is in danger, and you won't be able to protect yourself from further harm. You might try to suppress or ignore your trauma responses, because you've been taught that they were wrong. When you don't feel safe to express your emotions, your body stays in that stress response and you can end up with PTSD symptoms.

But if you have supportive people who can work through that trauma with you, you don't end up carrying or suppressing as many emotions and you're able to move forward a little easier.

If you're healing from abuse or trauma or a tough breakup, I hope this helps you feel a little less alone and helps you to forgive yourself. Abuse and mistreatment are never your fault, and you deserve support and understanding!

Thank you so much for supporting my book, and make sure to take breaks and check in with your emotions as you read, as this subject can understandably be difficult!

This Is Why I Never Left

Planting Guide

Throw out your collection
Of bottled-up fears,

And tend to your garden
Of shames and worries.

Do not allow them to overgrow,
Into your lilies of joy.

Water your hopes
And light a candle
To your everyday triumphs.

Let yourself be present,
Feel your feet touching the floor,
The pen across the page.

See the world
Through brand new eyes.

Notice how the light hits the trees,
How the shadows hover
Over the leaves.

Stretch your arms up like branches
Take up the space
You were never allowed

Climb to the top of the jungle gym
Run in the halls

Listen to the sound
Of the swings on the playground,

As you create new worlds
From the sand beneath the trees.

Make a friend,
Make a mistake,
Make it better.

Nature Vs. Nurture

They say all you need's a little water,
Little sunlight, and you're good to grow.

Nature versus nurture,
Who decides who we get to be?

Maybe some things can't be solved,
By a nice warm cup of tea.

How do you stop being afraid,
Of getting tangled in the vines?

Late night reminders,

It's going to take a little time,
And I won't bloom overnight.

But I see roots of something new,
Something brighter.

Citrus Roots

I come from the lemon city,
From the gazebo downtown.

"Did you know,
That the first lemon trees
In California were planted in 1709?"

I come from the stone city,
Where we'd jump over walls,
Just to paint our names in the hills.

I come from the trolley city,
A hidden landmark
Outside my favorite library.

I come from the children's section,
From colorful shelves,
And alphabet tiles.

"Where do you consider your hometown?"

I come from the chaparral city,
Where the mountains always point north.

Armor

Old photos sometimes feel
Like postcards from a different planet.
They never tell the story
Of how we got there, or why we left.

The holes in my jeans are a memory,

Of how I could never remember
To stop using the left door
Of your Nissan Leaf

Because the mangled metal
From all your accidents,
Would get caught on my jeans.

You were on speed dial,
Whenever I was stuck
At dark bus stops alone,

Because I knew you'd
Arrive faster than anyone.

You never could slow down,
Not even a traffic light
Could tell you what to do.

I post these photos like armor,
I don't want you to see what's underneath.

Love Poem: Island

I am the wind that grazes your hair,
The moon that lights your path.

As Aeaea was to Circe,
I'll be your safe harbor.

Here there are no rules to follow,
No Titans to serve.

Only friendly lions,
And the calling of birds.

If this were Ogygia you could stay
As long as you want.

And when you were ready,

I'd build you a raft,
To guide you home.

<u>Tidal Wave</u>

Anger doesn't always leave
When you throw a plate,
Or make a fist,

— It lingers

Among the shadows on the wall
And in the depths of the sea.

Left unchecked, it's a tidal wave,
That'll make its way to shore, eventually.

This Is Why I Never Left

Here, the grass rolls
Like it does in cartoons,

And the wind flings
You into new adventures.

Here, kind words
Form crystals on the ceiling.

And too close for comfort,
Is never close enough.

Wanting to believe,
Wanting to belong,

You don't see it,
Until it's too late.

Kindness,
Doesn't always
Mean safety.

And hospitality
Doesn't always
Mean you're home.

<u>Sagittaria</u>

"It's taken a lot of gardening in my heart, a lot of digging up so much soil and finding old roots that were in the way of other things blooming" -Hayley Williams

I spend so much time
Pulling up weeds.

Examining old beliefs,
Relationships, I thought
Would stitch me back together
Knit my synapses into a warm comforter.

But they just tore new holes,
And unraveled more loose threads.

People that pulled me into sections of time
I can't access
Doors cannot ~~will not~~ enter

My body buries them in the earth to protect me
But they threaten to flood my world,
Whenever it rains.

Parts of my body still feel like a dark lagoon

Sometimes I sit by the banks,
Lapping up water,
Tending to the earth.

Trying to listen for
What it wants me to learn

Sometimes the water lies still,
Sometimes it moves towards me,

Enveloping me in old emotions,
Old time periods,

Existing in two worlds,
I let it pull me in.

<u>Small Sparks</u>

I wish I could fold everything nicely,
And thank each memory
Before I let go.

I wish I could line up
My emotions
In neat little rows.

I want to make space for something new.
I want to open up the cupboards,
And the windows, to let in the sunlight.

I want to dust off my sheets
And place them safely inside,
The smell of rosemary and tide.

Turn Off The Moon And Unplug the Stars

Sometimes my body decides,
It's too light to stay on the ground.

Some days I'm a cloud,
Floating higher and higher,
Into the stratosphere.

Like a balloon
Someone couldn't hold.

I fall asleep on the moon,
And wake up in free fall.
A nebula of emotions,
Pink, green, sapphire, yellow.

Some days I'm full of rain,
And some days I can't catch my breath.

Sometimes I wake up on earth,
Thinking maybe if I leave the curtains closed,
The sun won't find me.

Seeking a Born Collaborator

Find me past the Snoopy and Woodstock mailbox,
We can go swimming
And I'll watch you climb trees.

They used to ask my parents
If I was quiet at home.

If I had friends,
If I was always alone.

They didn't see me at my loudest,
My silliest, at my lying in the street freeness.

When you read my diaries,
And tried on my sister's dresses.

You know, I'm starting to think
Collaboration is something learned,

Wading in the creek
With a hiking stick in hand.

Love Poem: Dandelion

The hills are my home.
I wave hello to the bees,
And watch over the tides.

I live among the cows
And the crocus.

I live among
Coffee shops and pigeons.

A fairy godmother of sorts,
I grant your every wish.

I've learned to be unafraid
Of new beginnings,

To feel at ease in
Empty valleys, and
Playgrounds filled with laughter.

And my only wish,
Is to bring a little magic
To the places I inhabit.

Graffiti and Skyscrapers

There is a safer world,
A summer of non-stop adventures,
Of venturing to the top of skyscrapers
Without a care in the world.

Days spent on the phone,
During long bus rides home.

And nights spent
Speeding down the mountain,
At 60 miles an hour.

When I think of mourning,

I remember days spent
Putting dishes in cupboards
Where they wouldn't be found.

And the days we clung
To each other.
We couldn't let go,
Even if we wanted to.

My therapist said it'd be good
To write our story down,
Little did she know I already had.

Our shaky hands gripping paint cans,
Knowing that even if they painted over our work,

We'd at least left some reminder that we were here.
A reminder of the years

We spent trying to feel alive.

When I think of forgiveness,
I hear running water,

And a helicopter nearing
As we climbed over the fence

You know, we never learned the difference
Between a boundary and a wall.

Mt. Baldy California, 2020

Porter-Kresge Road

Here,
The floor is covered in leaves,
And it's soft under my feet.

Here,
The deer cross the road,
We climb the trees,
And sometimes the traffic lights.

Turkeys and tamarins,
Owls and squirrels,
All ride the carousel
By the library.

We turn past the bridge,
And I know I'm home.

Queer Utopia

I live on the queer floor of my dorm,
Where everyone's bulletin boards

Are covered in rainbows,
And pronouns and Sanrio stickers.

I live a few steps away
From all my closest friends,

They bail me out every time I
Lock myself out of my room,

And the trans girl next door
Hosts movies nights, and super smash battles.

I choose jigglypuff every time.

We crowd into her room to
Watch Howl's Moving Castle,

We pour shots of vodka
Into Hello Kitty cups
Before karaoke night,

We take the bus downtown
To buy boba and plushies.

And Mondays are pizza party nights
Hosted by trans girls in the quad,
They don't ask us pay them back,
But I always buy them drinks and snacks,
Because I love them and I can.

We feed squirrels
Outside the dining hall.
We put pride flags in our windows,
And dye our hair silly colors
In the communal bathroom sink,

We sit in the meadow,
And watch the sunset over campus,

Trying to catch the last rays of light
Glistening over the ocean.

I Know Where the Summer Goes

In the morning,
There's a family of raccoons
Outside my window.

Four little raccoons looking
For breakfast in the bushes.

I start my day,
Walking down the ramp,
Past the two small deer
Grazing in the quad.

I turn into the dining hall,

Where someone has written

"Sixteen more days of summer session"

In big blue letters on the whiteboard in the hall

I stare up at letters
And remember when I was counting down

"Sixteen days 'til I get to move,"
Across the state to a little city in the hills,
That I'd only ever seen in brochures and dreams.

In sixteen days, everything's going to change again,
In sixteen days, the sunrises will come sooner,
And the air will get colder,

In sixteen days, everyone will leave

And I'll still be here, staring up at the sky.

Walking past my old dorm room,

Waiting sixteen days for it all
To start over again.

<u>Love Poem: Puddle</u>

Think of the body as
Something iridescent,

Reflecting the warmth of the pavement,
he clouds navigating the cool blue sky.

Show me your greatest fears,
Your greatest triumphs.

I know you are familiar with invisibility,
But resist the urge to camouflage.

We are here but a fraction of time,
And you deserve to feel whole.

I'll Give You a Year, I'll Give You a Lifetime

I make my home in the foothills of hope.
Where the sun returns to the sky,

And the clouds whisper, "*You belong here.*"

You squeeze my hand, and for a moment,
I almost believe it.

Lightyears

The sun turns around and brings us light.
Starting the countdown all over again.

When I open my eyes,
I watch the bus start its descent to the ocean,
And the soft purple light shining on your hoodie.

I have to say goodbye
To this safe seaside town soon,
And I have to say goodbye to you.

So instead of seashells,
I've been collecting stories,

Replaying all my conversations and adventures
Just so I could bring them back to you.

You told me you want to bring your camera everywhere,
To capture the light of each moment,
To follow it as it flickers through the trees,
And rests on the horizon.

Starting the day all over again.

Species-Being

*"Guide us / that we may learn / all the ways / to hold this tender this land." -
bell hooks, Appalachian Elegy*

But I am an environment too,
A whole ecosystem
Glowing in vibrant hues.

When we were kids,
When we were heroes,
We could feel it.

We would fill whole buckets,
And make castles from the earth.

You wear the crown,
And I'll wear the cape.

We'll keep searching,
Leaving marks in the earth.

Love Poem: Sandbox

If time is something nonlinear,
Why can I trace my steps from here to you,
And find all the places that made me this way?

I trace the line from the bushes
My friend pushed me into,
To the park where I grew up,
Racing cars on the freeway.

I can mark the spot where
I left my book on the playground,
Where they punished me for needing
To know what happens next.

These days, I still stack library books on my desk,
But I never make it to the ending.

Taurus Season

Have you ever heard
Of a bull that likes change?

Who steps lightly on the ground,
And likes honey in their tea?

A bull who sits by the stone wall thinking,

Maybe the grass is just greener
Where the sun shines.

Patient and impatient,
All at once.

I Don't Pray Anymore, But That Doesn't Mean My Heart's Out Of Prayers

Words have too much power
For what I'm trying to convey,

Let me be soft and gentle,
As my dad used to say.

Help me build something kinder
And smoother.

Help me sand all the edges,
And sweep away the debris.

A friend once asked me,
If I'm always striving to learn
Or always striving to be good

And I didn't have the heart
To tell her I'm still trying
To learn what goodness is.

All I know is,
Tenderness is a root,
Something that blossoms.

Every day I grow a little more,
And I see what I
couldn't before.

Let my apathy fall away,
Gently, like petals.

Let me sprout in the rain,
And find my voice
In the thunderstorm

The rainbow a promise,
That I'll try again tomorrow.

Park Bench

This time around,
I want to build a place
I don't have to run from.

You take my hand and say,
"I wish this happened sooner,"
And I say, *"I'm sorry it took me so long."*

Love Poem: Melody

Some days I want to find a reason,
A clashing note or a small thorn.
It shouldn't be this easy, right?

It always takes a minute,
For my fingers to find the melody,
to remember the notes,

But I feel so safe
When my hand's in yours.
It shouldn't be this easy, right?

I used to feel so scared
To ask for what I want,
But when I say, "*Come here,*"

I know I'll find you,
Sitting outside on the steps.

An Ode to the IKEA Shark (Blåhaj)

A jaw with no bite,
Fins with no oceans to cross.
Your own kind of lighthouse,
Bringing waves of warmth,
And soft blue velvet.

Get Me Away From Here, I'm Dying

"Thought there was love in everything and everyone / You're so naïve!" - Belle and Sebastian

I left my favorite blanket in New Mexico.
And a part of me in the redwood coastline of Santa Cruz.
The northern California fog became a part of me,
Until I learned the lesson, it followed me.

Driving across a red rock Arizona skyline.
I learned to trust the process,

Don't rush it.
Take as long as you need,

My favorite blanket,
A Christmas present,
From people I no longer talk to,

But the fabric was just right,
And it kept me warm and safe at night,

I wrapped my friends it in
Walking them back to their dorms,
When they got drunk late at night.

In San Antonio,
I took on
The prickly pear sting,
Of their words.

Social justice girlies
Are all about community,

Until your nervous system,
Needs a break,
And can't keep up the pace.

When going back for your
Favorite blanket,
Would inconvenience them too much.

I couldn't wait to be back home,
In my tiny 4th floor dorm.
Where staring up at redwoods,
Never gets old.

I tried to deal with it gracefully,
But I had to say goodbye to so much of me.
When I left my favorite blanket in New Mexico.

I tried to deal with it gracefully,
But I had to say goodbye to so much of me.

When I left my favorite blanket in New Mexico.

This is Graduation

When the grass sits yellow and still,
We pass on the torch
of what we cannot own.

A whole universe,
of daisy crowns and crying alone.

For Mehr

You were funny and brave
So smart, with a smile like an ocean wave.

The best of all of us,

A lionhearted leader,
Until she stole your crown.

Now there's a spot on her hand
She'll never be able to clean.

And she'll always be
More jester than queen.

She turned men into her puppets.
Because she wasn't brave enough

To take us down on her own.

We sat in that circle,
In a tiny dorm room

Confessing to sins
We had yet to commit.

I wish I had opened my door,
Kicked them out,

Just to let you in.

But time was ticking,
Betrayal sneaking

Over the horizon
Like a sinister sunrise.

It felt like I was
Watching everything

From the outside,

Like I wasn't sitting
In that room,

Waiting for the laughter
To stop.

Echo

Blink and you'll miss it
The stars outside the window
The trees swaying in the wind.

This isn't my first goodbye,
It's just an echo,
Of all my memories here.

This place was a fresh start,
A soft place to rest,
To heal, to love.

Blink and you'll miss it,
But I already do.

Ask Me Tomorrow?

I'm always
Understanding
Myself in reverse,

I know what I needed
Yesterday, a year ago,
Ten years ago,

But never
What I need today.

Shortcut

I wanted to be different
To erase all I am.

To start on a blank page,
A new stage.

A new cast of characters,
A new place to stay.

But you can't leave
The old place behind.

It lingers and paints everything,
In vibrant hues,
In old memories,
Old emotions.

Your body tries to guide the way,
But you still think you can outrun it.

Be the exception to the rule.

Thinking,

If I just try harder,
It won't end the same way,

I'll find the path
That makes it all go away.

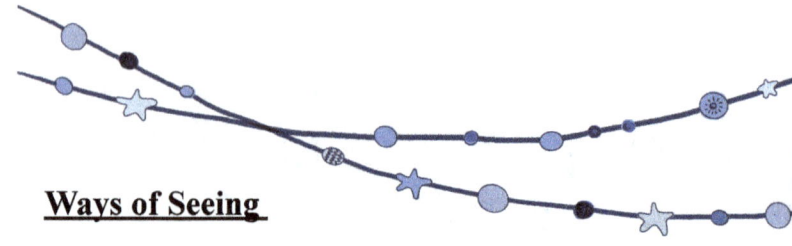

<u>Ways of Seeing</u>

The summer
After graduation
I sneak into the garden.

Lifting my camera
To the sky
Like I'd seen you
Do a thousand times.

Thinking, *What does*
The world look like from
Your point of view?

Capturing more than just light and leaves,
LEDs and sunsets sparkling,
Like the feeling of missing you.

Things That Aren't There Anymore

The fluorescent mall sign
That watched over our home

I used to beg my parents
To let me see it up close

Yelling, *"Luz del mol, luz del mol!"*

All my favorite childhood stores,
Gone since the recession.

Like the train car sitting by the freeway,
That greeted everyone coming down the off-ramp.

And the old, dilapidated house on our street corner
That I swore was haunted,
Torn down and rebuilt into a cookie-cutter-cabin.

My childhood playground,
Redesigned for the wealthier families,
And their dull grey houses.

And the old drive-in at the swap meet,
Where I'd prop my feet up on your dash,

Where I spilled horchata
All over his new shoes
And the back seat of his car.

They built a boring warehouse
Over our memories of popcorn and nachos,

And watching scary movies under the stars.

You know,

I wouldn't mind
The eerie twilight ride back home,
If I could just watch one more film in your car.
Order one more slushie.

Mars in the 4th House

I don't want to hate you,
But I don't know how to tell you
That my anger has never felt like mine.

It arrived here in a box
And I don't know its name.

My anger has roots like a redwood tree
With rings to count the years
And the passing of time.

I'm trying to remember
When this city didn't feel so sour
When it felt like a budding rose,
And a spoonful of honey.

Was there ever a time?

Maybe I've just forgotten.
The city that doesn't feel like home,
Only a memory.

Love Poem: Radio

I remember thinking,
If only I could get my voice
To the other side of this room.

If I could switch a wire or two
Find the place where
My voice is trapped,

Fix the short circuit,
And make my mouth run again

Like a department store playlist,
The same song over and over.

Change of City / Change of Heart

Sometimes people are better in microdoses,
In 300-mile-drives away,
In suitcase-and-a carry-on-distances.

Maybe absence
Makes the heart grow calmer,
And the vision clearer.

Banana Bread

My mom asks me to make
Banana bread muffins.

After she screamed at my dad,
And took his stuff,

(Threw it against a wall,
Or threw it away,
I don't remember which)

But I don't like bananas,
So, I make apple crumble muffins.

Not for her,
Not for him,
But for me.

Post-Traumatic Driver's Test

Having PTSD is like
Having a broken side-view mirror,

I see dangers that aren't there,
I misperceive the distance
Between me and other people.

I often stay in one lane for too long,
Never changing out of fear,
Of going in the wrong direction,

Sometimes it's easier
To just keep going forward.

Ignoring my internal GPS,
Telling me to make a U-Turn
At the next light,

Make a choice,
It tells me,
Any choice.

But it's like someone turned off
The headlights of my brain,
And I can't find the switch
To turn them back on.

Disguise / Desire

It shouldn't be a lot to ask
To not have to police
Or prune

To be loved
Without *struggle or epiphany*
As a bud in bloom.

"I feel safe with you," you say

Well,

It shouldn't be a lot to ask
For me to feel safe too.

<u>Say What You Mean</u>

"Truth, just like any other weapon, can act as an agent of oppression or a means of liberation, depending on who crafts the narrative." -Ismatu Gwendolyn

I'm always deciphering,
Finding the meaning

Behind his words,

Because he never says
What he means.

Or means what he says.

"Do you want to go home?"

Translation: He wants to go home.

And sometimes,
I can he doesn't feel well,
But he won't tell me:

*"Do you have a headache?
Should we sit inside?"*

He manipulates me to be on guard for
His unmet needs, because he
Communicates them to me.

*"I love you
I feel safe with you"*

Translation: Say it back
Translation: I'm creating
The illusion of safety,
Of trust, when there's really
Nothing to find.

He says, *"I can try..."*
He just thinks that's
What I want to hear.
But he won't,
He's told me so many lies
That I don't even know
What I want anymore,

Maybe all I want
Is for him
To stop talking.

To stop waiting
To hear his voice
Over the phone.

<u>A Fond Farewell</u>

"I can deal with some psychic pain if it'll slow down my higher brain" - Elliott Smith

Farewell to a dream I once held,
Farewell to the safety
I thought I had found.

Farewell to the redwoods
And the fog's soft embrace.

Farewell to 60-degree summers,
And deer on every trail.

Farewell to koi ponds,
And movie nights.

Farewell to tiny dorm rooms,
And long flights of stairs.

Farewell to comp sci majors,
And creepy forest paths.

Farewell to lighthouses,
And stoners on every corner.

Farewell to sunsets on the squiggle,
And bus rides down the coast.

Turns out there's more to the Bay,
Than bridges and flower crowns.

Farewell to gentrifiers,
And tech bros on every corner.

Farewell to surfers and floods,
Farewell to banana slugs,
Lounging in the mud.

Farewell to grind culture,
Farewell to steep sidewalks
And spooky Victorian homes.

Farewell to sea lions lounging at the pier,
And coyotes lurking in the dark.

Farewell to midnight trips
To Safeway and Ferrell's

Farewell to dutch crunch bread,
And screaming college kids
"I'm trying to go to bed!"

Farewell to dining hall chicken sandwiches,

And soft serve machines.

And farewell to friends who never called,
Who never cared,
To check if you were okay.

Farewell to friends who weren't there,
To hold you through
Your very first breakup.

Farewell,
Farewell.

Dressing Room

Girls who hate themselves
Always hate me.

They weave themselves into me,
Like vindictive frenemies,

They keep their self-hating
Suffocating energy
In the pockets of their jeans.

Saving it for just the right moment,
Just the right girl who doesn't fit
their narrow definitions of worth,

They stitch into my collarbone,
Like an enveloping coat over my shoulders
Pulling the wool over my eyes.

"It would totally look good on you,
Why don't you try it on?"

Both Sides Of The Story

But I need privacy too,
Did you think of that when
You told her all my secrets

And never let me read the words?
What's worse than knowing
Is not knowing,

What did you tell her?
What advice did she give you?

She knew your side, but what about mine?
It only lives in my mind
and the pages of journals I folded into origami cranes.

Your side of the story,
A side I'll never get to know.

A side wrapped in the lies she told me.
The unwanted hints
She tried to drop into my lap,

With her I-know-more-than-you-smile,
When she shouldn't have known
Anything at all.

There's comfort in familiarity,
In pretending I don't know
Just to keep the peace.

There's no stability,
In transformation,

No safety in destruction,
But where's the fun in staying the same?

Things I Like About New York

Emerging from a subway stop into a brand-new place
Dogs in puffer vests
The girl who jumped the turnstile then turned around to
open the door for me, seconds before the train took off

Things I Don't Like About New York

The sound of the elevator in my sister's building when it
gets to each floor
The way my shoelaces untie every few minutes

The record store employee who keeps trying to get me to
look at the CDs behind the counter - "Leave your stuff, stay
for a while" "Have I seen you before?" "You free tonight?"

Things I Like About New York

The CDs I bought as an excuse to leave the store, New
Wave for me, Billie Holiday for my sibling and 70s hits for
my mom
Taking the train one stop just to avoid Times Square
Christmas markets in Bryant Park

Things I Don't Like About New York

The stores with tiny claustrophobic aisles - saying "sorry,
excuse me" over and over
The guy at the party who puts his hand on my knee as he
gets up from the couch
Motorcyclists who drive on the sidewalk

Things I Like About New York

People playing live music on every corner

Eating bagels and walking in central park
The way the leaves fly in the wind

Things I Don't Like About New York

Zoning out and missing my subway stop
Feeling sore from walking all day
Getting used to the time change

Things I Like About New York
That I'm 2,923 miles away from you

Things I Don't Like About New York
That I'm 2,923 miles away from you

Science Hill Bridge

There's still a space in me,
Where the concrete blocks the light.
Where flowers won't grow,

Where I can't feel anything bloom.

I don't know how to care for her,
How to give her what she needs,

A disconnect,
A crack in the sidewalk,

A distance
I can't bridge.

You know, I still cry when I see redwood trees,
They make me feel homesick,
For a place I never fully got to grieve.

Sitting under the shade of those trees,
Makes me feel like
I'm falling in and out of love
All over again.

Makes me think of the trees
That lead to the bridge,

Where I stopped you from jumping,
And walked you home at midnight,
In the dark of the forest.

You were so drunk
You could barely stand.

And I stayed on your floor,
Because I couldn't walk home,
Couldn't face the coyotes howling alone.

Sometimes I wonder
What would have happened if
I hadn't been there,

And I think about
How often I'd bite my tongue,
Fearing that one wrong word,
Would send you over the edge,

And how scared I was
That no one would be there to stop it.

Then sometimes, I think about how
I was so busy trying to save you,
I couldn't see the danger I was walking into.

But He's So Nice

"As other girls prayed for handsomeness in a lover, or for wealth, or for power, or for poetry, she had prayed fervently let him be kind" - Anais Nin, *A Spy in the House of Love*

December,
A lifetime away from where we began
Running in circles
Veiling your lies, by blaming me.
Oh, she's crazy, she's got no boundaries!

But every accusation's
A confession, because
You can't set a boundary
To save your life.

You want to be the hero
Who saves everyone

But is it out of genuine care,
Or a burning resentment?

That stays hidden
Until it spins out of control.

A coward in
More ways than one

Never the golden child,
Just the burdened son.

Christmas in Palestine

Children don't ask to be martyrs.
But Santa can't get into Gaza
Because the walls are too high.

He doesn't have the right visa,
And there are too many checkpoints to cross.

The olive trees beckon him to land below,
And the settlers drive him out with tear gas and tanks.

There's no Christmas in Bethlehem this year,
Their hearts are too full of mourning,
To hang up the stars, the twinkling lights
That guide the wise men and their gifts.

And all the men wearing crowns,
Are too busy, counting coins
To put presents under the tree.

Love in the Time of Genocide

I turn on the news and
      Wake up dreaming of bombs
And shattering glass.

A week goes by,
      1 month,
            2 months,
            4 months.

I turn off the news
      And dream of falling stars

Of white phosphorus
      And shrapnel.

How many more days?
      Another week
            Another month
            Another year?

Then all the lies I believed
      To stay in your orbit

            Suddenly fall apart

      Like the lies we tell
            To uphold empire.

12th House Moon

I wish I could,
Confide in you

But I don't want to

be shaped by
your point of view.

Maybe a part of me will
Always feel like
A small child,

I carry her
with me still.

Reluctantly,

A part of me
May always feel
Safer in isolation

Whispering
It's over,
   It's over,
      It's over.

The Princess Loses Her Voice In This One

The last time I was in San Diego,
I watched from a distance,

Letting the tide wash you away,
Thinking I've heard this story before,
I know how it ends.

Maybe I let go
A long time ago,
And I was holding on
because it was all I knew.

Your voice,
A net trapping me,
In an ocean of shame.

Then one day the choppy waters below
Turned crystal blue.

The distance
An ocean,
We never intended to cross.

But knowing and accepting
Are two different things.

And running and staying
Are often the same.

Maybe it isn't about
Finding something that was lost,

But about holding onto

Something that was never there.

You'd said I'd be safe here,
So why does leaving you feel
Like coming home?

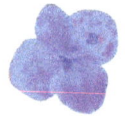

Until you're drowning in the whirlpool Of emotions they expect you to carry your Body, a sensory lifeguard reeling you in. When you've wandered too far from shore. Until you can't tell the Difference between the water and your own Body. It isn't safe to Swim. The water is stronger than you think, And there's a sea monster you won't see until It's pulled you in. Like falling water. But enmeshment Isn't depth. It's a poison. It's a prison. You shouldn't dive in. You see through others. You sense their feelings, Running your hands over them You wanted to Be seen the way. You

I Consider Him To Be

Once, my friend told me
A boy she dated was a rapist
She said it so nonchalantly,

I consider him to be

So, I believed her.

I grew up with him,
I remembered how he stared at me
A little too long,

I brushed it off because it made me feel ashamed,
Even though I was a child and did nothing wrong.

I remembered at summer camp
When he told me
Everything was about "the wrong spot," everything.

When women come forward,
They tell us we're ruining his public image,

But I think we're just trying to make it clearer,

Make him easier to spot,
Before he harms someone else,
And acts like it was a one-time thing.

A small mistake, not a calculated effort.
Because he thought we'd stay quiet,
That we wouldn't know better.

I consider him to be

That's how I learned it didn't matter,

What *his* intentions were,
What sweet words fell from his coercive mouth,
When you tried to say no,
When you tried to back away.

One small mistake,
Will never cover
The personality he faked,
The secrets and texts he hid
Because he knew
You would never say yes
If you knew.

I consider him to be

Though we don't talk anymore,
I wish I could have called her
Time and time again,

Just to say

"I know what you mean now. You're not crazy,
You're just high off the taste of male validation,

And the promise of finally being cared for,
Finally, being seen"

Everything I tried to tell her while we were friends
Even though it didn't change a thing.

I tried to avoid it for as long as I could,
But then it happened to me.

I consider him to be
I believe me.

I just wish we weren't told that men hold
Our worthiness in the palm of their hands,

Because maybe then we would have found it,
In our own clenched fists.

The Anger Never Left Me

"Sometimes rage feeds you when nothing else will" - Kai Cheng Thom, *Falling Back In Love With Being Human*

I always took it with me,
Like a stamp
On my fifth grade
Report card,

"I don't know if
she just has no respect
For authority or what"

The anger never left me,
it followed me
Like a heavy cloud of smoke,

A fire
I couldn't put out.

The anger never left me,
But that didn't stop me
From trying to outrun it.

The anger never left me,
It took center stage.

I tried to run from my rage,
And all I got was more rage.

Quiet, Girl

"Some days I want to spit me out, the whole mess of me, but mostly I am good and quiet." Camille Rankine, Emergency Management

So, if there's no thorns out there,
Maybe I should check my own hands.

I used to hold my fears so tightly,
They burned holes through my coat,
And turned my fingers red.

A thousand apologies laced up in my shoes,
But the words can never come untied.

I'm scared I won't forgive myself.

Scared to be anything more
Than the quiet girl,
With her hands in her pockets.

Manipulators

They turn your intelligence into arrogance,
Your kindness into weakness,
Your vulnerability into a weapon
To hide their own shame.

Your light becomes too bright for them,
Your effort not enough for them.
And your values become a trap
For them to lure you in.

But the mirror slowly turns back on them
Their lies begin to reflect who they are
Until they realize you're no longer afraid of them.

They have no power once you let go
Of the fear and the guilt of being the villain
In their twisted version of the story.

You have to stay steady
Like an unbending oak tree
Never faltering, never wavering
Taking in all their carbon dioxide
And transmuting it into oxygen

Filling their lungs like
They filled you with their own inadequacy
You are the air that they breathe.

Scream and cry
For as long as you need

Until you can say,

"Misery loves company
Guess that's why I'm only happy
When they're far away from me."

Never Again

"The longer I live, the more deeply I learn that love–whether we call it friendship or family or romance–is the work of mirroring and magnifying each other's light…lifesaving work in those moments when life and shame and sorrow occlude our own light from our view, but there is still a clear-eyed, loving person to beam it back." - James Baldwin

I'm ruled by the sun,
Guess I was chasing
My own shadow,
Like a snake biting its own tail.

Because you had no fuel to run.
No light to beam back.

Small

Every dream I chase
Wakes the part of me
That wants to run.

The part of me that
Wants to play small,

That wants to shrink
To fit into every outdated
Idea of who I should be.

But staying small
Only ever leads to resentment,

Pretending you have no needs,
And denying what you know,
Only makes your feelings stronger,

Only puts you at war
With your own senses,
With your own mind.

There's no prize for
Fitting yourself into tiny crevices,
For chasing after scraps
Of affection and approval.

All you do is get smaller,
Your appetite gnawing,
Your hunger growing,
Until it devours you whole.

King of Swords (Reversed)

When I moved back,
I had to re-learn how to eat.

When I left you,
I had to re-learn how to speak.

"You used to be so skinny"

My mom tells me,

"Why were you so skinny?"

Well,
It just didn't
Feel safe
To be me.

Maybe my body,
Was only trying
To tell me

To flee,
To get out
And never
Look back.

She says,

"Okay well,
Just make sure
You don't eat
Too much.

Lessons

A lot of people think / that hitting and screaming at / their children is a good form of discipline / or that it teaches them a lesson / and that is crazy to me.

Abuse / doesn't teach / children to be better / it just destroys our self esteem / and makes us scared / of conflict and making mistakes. / Because / we were taught / that if we do something wrong / we deserve to be hurt / and punished / so we run from accountability / and admitting when we've messed up.

We make better choices / when we feel good about ourselves / when we can trust ourselves / to make good decisions / and repair our relationships. / But abuse / completely destroys / our trust in ourselves / and in other people.

Abuse will never teach / your child to hold themselves accountable / it will only make them feel / like they deserve / to be mistreated and abused / or worse / teach them / that it's okay / to mistreat other people.

Affirmations For Accessing Healthcare in the US:

I love begging doctors to do their job!
I have faith in the American healthcare system!
Being put on hold by insurance companies is genuinely fulfilling!
I did not have to change my primary care doctor 3 times this week!

Yes, I've tried therapy!
Yes, I've tried birth control!
Yes, I've tried SSRIs!
Can you run the test anyway?
Even if you think there's nothing to find?

No, I don't need a psych eval,
No, I don't want to try another anxiety med.
No, I don't have an eating disorder...
Okay, maybe I have an eating disorder,
But I asked for help maybe 20 times before I developed an eating disorder!

"Your test results are fine!
You're young, you're healthy.

This sounds like anxiety,
"How's it going in therapy?"

"As you did it / to the strangest of my sisters / you did it to me." - Emily Austin, Gay Girl Prayers

<u>Even If I Was</u>

The weirdest,
         Most unlikeable
                  Undesirable
Girl on the planet,

                  I still wouldn't deserve
                           To be treated like this.

I still deserved, a kinder ending,
An honest apology,

                  Not a guilt ridden
                           "Sorry I got caught."

Society still wants
         Perfect victims,

They let you don't make mistakes
                  Or defend yourself from abuse or oppression
                           Or show up imperfectly in relation-
         ships.

         When you finally escape,
                  A place so unsafe,
                           You crash out,
                           You're

crazy! No wonder he left.

We love to look for a reason
Not to care,
Not to empathize.

Anything to feel the relief of turning
away,
From the violence we enable.

And if we admit that women
Are complex and
flawed
Not always right,
Not always innocent
Not always tiny and pure,

Then we end up caught up
in the myth of deservingness.

But I don't need to throw
Other girls under the bus
Just to prove
I'm capable
Likable,
Desirable.

Because nothing will ever
Make me,
Make anyone
Deserving of abuse.

And I'd rather be crazy
Than complicit.

For The Lover Girls

No more swallowing anger,
Just to be polite.

Neglecting all your needs,
Just to prove you're not uptight.

They tell you,
Take the high road.

Stroke his ego,
Take the fall,
Take one for the team.

Don't you know
He's just blowing off steam?

You give up your
Power, your dreams.
And they tell you
It's worth it

But what has
The high road
Ever gotten you?

When they go low,
Take out the whole damn road

The Revolution Starts at Home

My body shakes off trauma / a little too easily / and I don't mean that in a "Ehh that happened but I turned out okay" kind of way / I mean that in an understanding my nervous system / and why it chose a particular trauma response in that situation / "Okay well I literally just felt unsafe / and my body was trying to protect me in the only way it could" / That's over now / I got myself out of it / and I'm not always the problem / that person had major issues / and maybe I do too / but at least I'm working on them / and I probably always will be / because I don't have the luxury / of ignoring / my trauma responses / because they impact / every second of my life / and I don't have / the patriarchal privilege / that lets me mistreat every marginalized person around me / and still have a career / and a community of people who think I'm a great guy / and I'm kind of always in perpetual danger / in account of looking like / a sixteen-year-old-girl / with a sweet face / and kind eyes / like I'm easy to take advantage of / and manipulate / kind of way.

Good Luck

I open my friend's Instagram story to a
Rainbow color meme that reads:

"You're in his DMs, I'm trying to unlearn
What he made me hate about myself. Good luck!"

The words transport me back to a city by the sea,

Holding his hand, walking into town from the bus stop.

When someone rushes past us on a bike yelling
"Love never lasts, good luck with that one!"

Sparks shot through my hand
The first time he held it
Like the buzzing of an electric fence,

Warning me to stay away.

I'm Almost Glad It Happened

Because now I understand
Now I can relate,
I have my own shitty ex stories

To share with friends
To break the ice,
To connect with people
The way I could
Never connect with you.

Laughing at midnight
In the booth
Of a Mexican restaurant.

"And then what happened?"
"Oh, girl, you still stayed?"

I forgot I could laugh that way,
Beaming as the story that left my lips
Became a silly tale,
Another awkward moment survived.

Not the earth-shattering-world-altering-
perspective-bending-heartbreak it had been the year before.

I'm almost glad it happened,

Illusions shattering like glass slippers,
Turning you from a pretend prince into pumpkin,

Running back to myself
As the clock struck midnight.

Singing along to Britney,
She said, *"Cinderella's got to go!"*

I'm almost glad it happened,
But what I still can't ignore,

Is how all the blood in my veins
still strains to circulate,

How it struggles to bring oxygen to my brain.
All the dizzy spells,

That took over my mind
From trusting your voice over mine.

I'm almost glad it happened,

Because now I know,
What I want and what I'll never accept,

Now I know what no feels like,
And what suppressing it
Does to the beating in my chest.

I'm almost glad it happened,

I got so comfortable crying,
It started to feel soothing,
Instead of like stinging nettles,
Piercing my skin.

I'm almost glad it happened,

Because you inspired me
To be nothing like you.

I wanted to prove
I could feel my emotions,

And hold space for them
Like you never could.

I'm almost glad it happened,

Because I think everything
Played out the way it should.

if the body keeps score, maybe places do too

AVOID AVOID AVOID

Love Poem: Wanderer

Most days I feel
Like an unsent letter.

I'm covered in ink,
And I've run out of postage stamps.
Wouldn't it be better to land,
Than to call the sea your home?

Somedays the mist
Feels like a looking glass,

You can look out from your pile
Of crumpled papers,
And spot an island.

By now you've done
This a dozen times,

You arrive ashore,
And spot a jaguar, and a monkey.

You wonder how anyone
Could ever call this place deserted.

The plants in the grove race on
An expedition to the top
Of the mountains.

Here, there's no need
For translation,

And the birds already
Know our names.

Halloween

It's Halloween,

And I don't want to wear a mask anymore
I don't want to think of myself as scary, or haunted.

I want to be the cool breeze,
The smell of cinnamon sugar
Something warm, and comforting.

It's Halloween and I'm done with tricks,

No more hiding my words behind colors and chords,
I want to be tangible like a falling leaf.
I want to stick around even in winter, or spring.

"Why aren't you dressed up?"

My third grader teacher asked
As I sat in the corner away from
The other princesses in my class.

We always hid in the house on Halloween,
It was the Devil's holiday,

We never left candy outside,
Only closed blinds and a dark front porch.

The Window Seat

It still feels like
I'm healing wrong,
Bent out of shape.

I keep wondering.
If the body keeps the score,
What if places do too?

I told myself
Hide yourself
Away until it's safe.

But what's the point
Of the window seat
If I'm staring at the ground?

For Shelly and Sanai

I was there when the boys made you cry,
I met you by the gate and
Brought ice cream to school.

I was in there in the shopping cart,
You pushed down the hill.

I was there on your fifteenth birthday,
Eating pizza and
Playing table hockey all night.

I was there on weekends with your dad
Sneaking handfuls of popcorn
Upstairs in our pockets,

When your grandmother
Said to eat in the kitchen.

I was there on weekdays with your mom,
Playing wii sports, and talking
To strangers online.

I was there at your sweet sixteen,
In dresses and heels,
In the middle of the dance floor.

At homecoming, at prom,
At Denny's at 3 am.

I was there on trips to LA,
When your brother would drive,
Because your mom hated the freeway.

I was there on vacations,
Driving golf carts in circles,
And driving the old folks crazy.

I was there at the drive-in,
Watching movies and
Sitting in the trunk staring at the sky.

And I was there when you
Where nowhere to be found,
Texting updates to your sister,
Making sure you were safe.

I was there at graduation,
Flipping tassels in the air.

I was there when we threw
Your eighteenth birthday party
In my backyard,

Set up a jumper and everything,
Under the stars.

I was there when
Your mom moved away,
When your dad
Got his own place to stay.

I was there at your twentieth birthday party,
Spilling drinks on my socks and the carpet.

I was there at Halloween parties,
At beer pong tables, and mountain drives.

I was there on door dash runs,

And the times we'd dress up
To get sushi just for fun.

I was there at twenty-two,
Catching up before I moved to school,
Like no time had passed by at all.

I was there when you turned twenty-four,
Brought you balloons,
That your dog tried to fight.

And I should've told you
What happened that night,

My shitty partner made me sad,
Tipsy and hiding in the bathroom,
Because I wasn't ready to talk it out just yet.

But you were there when it ended,
Not so out of the blue,
But still just as painful,
What else is new?

I was there walking your dog
Around the block.
I was there keeping you company,
On the clock,

I was there when
She was diagnosed,
I was there when she
had her first surgery,

I was there when you both turned twenty-five,
Canceled the party,

Because she didn't feel fine.

I was there when you started chemo
And when it started to spread
I was there next to your hospital bed.

Your sister told me,
"All our best memories are with you"

So just hold on a little longer,
Just stay with me.

I promise,
I'll be there,
I'll be there,
I'll be there.

Tired

I'm tired of sending letters,
Of signing petitions.

I'm tired of
Of asking my government
To save my life,
To save my friends lives,

Save the lives
Of people I don't know
People I've never met,
I'm tired of screaming
On the internet.

I'm tired of
Posting go-fund me
Links online
Like it'll save the world.

I'm tired of
Calling governors
Who couldn't care less.
Congressmen who leave us on read.

I'm tired of inboxes full
Of tired people begging for help.

I'm tired of watching
Preventable crisis
After preventable crisis,

Mishandled,
Misconstrued,

By powerful people
Who just weren't in the mood,

To do more, to say more,
To stop more.

I'm tired of writing grant applications,
Of competing for help,
Of proving that I'm deserving of care.

I'm tired of donating to nonprofits,
That embezzle funds
But won't pay their workers
A livable wage.

Liberation may not happen
In my lifetime,
But could it speed up a little?

My friends are dying,
The planet's dying,

Sent, and delivered.

Not An Academic

I'll never be
Entirely neutral,
Objective,
Logical,
Or theoretical.

I'll never be
A minimalist,
I feel everything
At once.

Guess that makes
Me an artist,

— Not an academic.

But I'm also
So tired of feeling,

Like that makes
Me less analytical,
Less intelligent.

It Started At Lunch Time

Sitting by your side,
Sometimes under the tree,
Sometimes by building C.

I first met you in junior high,
You were in my P.E. class,
Until you dislocated your knee.

We didn't become friends until
Sophomore year, we had
Our own inside jokes,
Our own little world.

It started as the three of us,
Until she got tired of us,
Started chasing boys,

Tried to tell her she deserved more,
But she never wanted my advice.

She wasn't satisfied without
A ring around her finger,
A man to call her own.

Sitting on her couch, she told me
"Love means sacrifice."

By the time she got married,
I'd moved away,

I didn't come to the wedding,
Because we weren't on speaking
Terms anymore.

And I always felt like the villain,
For trying to help her see her worth,
But she took mine in the process.
Made me feel like dirt.

She told me I was
Unlikeable, undesirable
Because I didn't enjoy going
On dates every night.

It was a choice I made to
Protect myself,
But she turned it into a weapon
To quell her own shame.

One of the last things she
Said, before I left was,

*"You know I'll move on from this,
But what about you?"*

Should've known it
Was just manipulation,

A way to make up
For her own perceived
Shortcomings, or a fear
That a ring would never
Sit on her finger,

That she'd be the one
Left alone, unchosen.

What she doesn't know is,
That single women are the

Happiest demographic.

And I never liked men at all,
I mean tried to,
To satisfy everyone else's desires,

But I lost myself
in the process…

It started at lunchtime,
Sitting by your side,
Sometimes under the tree,
Sometimes by building C.

I first met you in junior high,
You were in my P.E. class,
Until you dislocated your knee.

You've been out since junior high,
I've been confused since always.

You always understood me,
But it took me a while to see,
Who I was, and time to untangle it
From who they wanted me to be.

I Wrote This When I Woke Up From Anesthetics

Sometimes I miss the safety of her room

Her dad didn't allow boys in her room
(Well, at least not while he was home)

So, her room became my hiding place,
When she'd bring over her army of guys,
And expect me to keep her safe,
Keep her in line.

Her dad didn't say anything,
About how she let me cry in her room
After the worst day at my first job.

Or the time my mom dropped me off
On the side of the road when she was upset
So, I walked to her house until my mom came back.

I always washed the dishes and left the place clean.
Her home was my safe place away from home,

And she knew that,
So, I was the one she'd call
When a boy left her on read,
Or mistreated her again.

I spent hours watching movies on her TV,
Working on anthropology assignments in her room,
Because she couldn't be alone, and I couldn't stop working.

Just an empathetic overachieving, academic
And a girl who blurred the lines so much,

I couldn't untangle her life from mine,
Her wants from mine.

Until I finally had to end it,
I woke up to 29 missed calls
On my answering machine

Pressing play to hear, "You're just like everyone else, they always leave."

Doctor's Orders

I told my mother
I was scared to go to the gynecologist.

She told me that was
what I got for my stupid decisions.

But you know what?

Spare me the lesson,
I will not listen to someone
whose values are so tangled,
So twisted,

So laced with outdated misogyny,
And a self-hating fear
That I'll fall out of line.

Because I get shamed for not dating men,
And then I get shamed
For the men "I choose."

When I'm thriving on my own,
It should just be temporary

I mean, *who is going to take care of me?*

Crying in the car
On the way home from therapy,

I tried to find the words to tell them,
What if I don't want a man?

I mean, he'd probably only take care of himself

Or resent me for his self-centered
Attempt of providing.

No, I guess you can't win in a system,
that doesn't want you to exist.

So, I'll bite my tongue
Endure the pain and
Ignore my body once more,

Because I'm scared
To go to the gynecologist.

Santa Cruz California

2021-2022

Dear Keren,
 I had so much
fun being your
teacher. I will always
remember what a good
reader you are!! You
always drew a blue
bunny on every
picture so I could
tell which picture was
yours!
 Good luck in
first grade.
 Love,
 Mrs. Lewis

2005♡

Japanangeles

Saturday, 11 am.
Taking the A train to
Little Tokyo.

I meet my friends in the plaza,
Under lanterns and bonsai trees.

We catch up over ramen,
And coffee,
Retail therapy,
And claw machines,

We take silly selfies,
On disposable cameras,
And dance in the store aisles.

My friend smiles
As he tells every cashier,

"I bought this for my boyfriend,
I love my boyfriend,
Can't wait 'til he sees this,

Oh, he's going to love it!

My boyfriend,
My boyfriend,
My boyfriend!"

Donde Quepan Muchos Mundos

"Finally, I can admit: I dream of care that has nothing to do with survival." -
Jody Chan, Impact Statement

I want a sunlit room
— Which is to say,
I want you near me.

I want to feel connected,
Which is to say I want to
Feel separate.

I want to be my own person,
With my own needs.

I want to be with people,
Who don't make me
Feel like I have to ask
For permission to breathe.

I want agency to spread my wings and fly,
And a shoulder to cry on when I need it.

In our hands,
Loaves of bread will multiply.

— Which is to say we
Are our own miracle.

Love Poem: Canopy

Layer by layer, I'll find you.
Your heart is a jungle.
And I'm a clear blue lake,
You see right through me.

As Seen On TV

"Who can I become in such a world where the meaning and limits of the subject are set out in advance for me?" - Judith Butler

I used to watch a lot of reality TV,
Trying to figure out
Who I was supposed to be,
What I was supposed to want.

I cheered for the girls
To get their happy ending,
Or begged them to leave
From behind my screen.

But can love really bloom,
On a show that makes no room
To challenge oppression,
Or really get to know someone,
Before you commit to them?

Is it true love?
Or just a neoliberal dream
Of acceptance and security?

Because love isn't about
Tolerating or ignoring differences.
Or pretending they aren't there.

And it isn't about
Sacrifice or betraying
Yourself as a sign of care.

What if we had the agency
To be the full messy, complex

Versions of ourselves
In our society.

Would we need all these fantasies?
Places to escape
Or romantic fairy tales?

We all need to be seen,
And we all deserve care
But there must be
Something more,

There must be
Another way.

Something beyond
The nuclear family
Picket fence dreams
They keep trying to sell us.

I mean,
Maybe love's just about
Being around the people,
Who make you feel the most free.

If You've Been Paying Attention

You'd know the difference / between marginalized people / and privileged groups / is that we're / usually conscious / of the masks we're wearing / I know when I'm holding back my anger / and editing my personality / to fit into white spaces / changing myself / to be more palatable / But white people / and other privileged groups / don't know / there's a mask at all / or they simply refuse to acknowledge / that it's there.

They get so mad / when we break / their false decorum / when we won't defer to them / It feels like disrespect to them / but we're just revealing them / for who they really are.

They're violent / with smiles on their faces / and when we dare / to call them out / we're labeled / disrespectful / undeserving / ungrateful / and put in our place / It makes you feel crazy / when folks who seem nice / on the surface / are also / actively / knowingly / stabbing you in the back.

Marginalized people / are always blamed / for being divisive / but if you've been paying attention / the people in power / have been incredibly disingenuous / and oppressive all along.

Like The Birds

"It benefits no one to live in a world where these things happen,"
-Suzanne Collins, Mockingjay

Beyond the prison walls,
There's the most beautiful world.

Ponds full of moss and dragonflies.
Ducks floating above the surface,
Lounging under willow trees,
Calling to each other and searching for food.

I watch a little duck dive under the surface,
Following a school of minnows.

The duck stays under a little too long,
And I start to wonder if it'll ever come back up.

Moments later,
I see the duck rise to the surface
And my breath returns.

I watch the duck glide effortlessly over the surface,
Unaware I was ever worried,
Unaware of any danger,
Just focused on the tasty treats hiding in the moss.

This little pond,
Hidden between warehouses,
And prison gates,
Feels like a miracle.

Like if I tried to find it again,
It would just disappear.

The ducks don't know about the gates
That lie just beyond their little paradise.

Their homes replaced with so-called rehabilitation.
How can a landscape hold such contradiction?

The free birds swimming and flying with ease,
Mere feet from gates that keep so many loved ones in.

The hills are filled with flowers,
Yet the yard outside
The gates remains bare.

It's like the earth knows what was taken,
It sits in waiting for the day
It can reclaim its own body.

When its people are set free,
Like the birds.

Abolish Silicon Valley

"There's this term social entrepreneurship that I see tossed around a lot these days...if our "solutions" are just tinkering within the system, how can we truly imagine, let alone build, a better world?" - Dean Spade

I used to sit in classrooms,
Where they told us tech was the future,
Like we were on the cusp

Of something great,
Something revolutionary.

If tech was on a spectrum from inherently
Evil to inherently good,
It must lie somewhere in the middle.

It's neutral,
Just a tool,
We get to decide
How it's used.

"I swear the internet's cool!"

It's not turning your kids into
Rebellious monsters,
Or self-absorbed fools.

It's better to give kids the tools,
To learn for themselves,
To make up their own minds,
Then to try to hide them,
Shield them from ideas we despise.

But what our teachers didn't tell us
Is that there are kids in the Congo

Digging their tiny hands in the earth,

Mining lithium while we
Run our mouths online.

I see their tiny hands,
And tired eyes, every time
I turn on my phone.

Now I sit in classrooms
Wondering,

Why we call tech
Liberatory,
Revolutionary

When there are children
Dying around the globe
Just so we can learn how to code.

Gen Z

"Reporters & fathers call your generation 'the worst.' Which really means 'queer kids who could go online & learn that queer doesn't have to mean disaster"' - Chen Chen

Children were never your
Objects to own.

Not your trophies,
Or a mid-life milestone.

We were canaries in a coal mine
Trying to tell you it was time

Time to stop ignoring us
Punishing us
Tearing us down
In your headlines.

One of the most politically
Active generations

No, we were not
Hopeless or apathetic.

But we were the ones to blame
For the mental health epidemic.

They told us it was our phones
Restricted the internet,
Told us it was just teenage hormones,
That we'd understand when we got older.

But how were we
Supposed to grow up
Without feelings of despair,
In a world full of adults
who didn't care?

They used us
As a rhetorical argument,
A scapegoat for all
Society's problems.

Children are the future,
So, we have to keep them
Off the street
And out of our way.

It never matters if their
Bellies are full,
As long as they behave.

You know the highest rates
Of mental health issues,
Aren't from the internet,

They're from abuse
And neglect, something

We all claim to be against
But we never take credit for.
No, we never take steps to correct.

Kids' lives are not just
Sob stories to collect,
Or statistics to recite,
Something to apologize for

In hindsight.

You can't say
We didn't warn you
What continues is what
You condone.

But hey, what do I know?
Maybe it's just that damn phone.

Fight

I fight and
I fight and
I fight.

I've fought so hard
I've lost sight,

Of who I could be
If I just allowed myself
To stop fighting.

To let things be,

To just listen to
That little voice inside me

Whispering,

"I want to live,
I want to live,
I want to live!"

Sometimes I can't tell
If I'm fighting her,
Or if she's fighting me.

They always tell me to
Ignore her,
  Neglect her,
    Suppress her,

But I'm learning to
Nurture her,

Raise her,
 Protect her,

Drowning out
All the voices
surrounding me

Until it's just
Me and my angry
Inner child.

Me and the rage
I can't drown out.

Me and the bravest
Girl I know.

Guiding me,
Telling me,

"I think I can accept
What happened to me,

But I won't forgive,
I won't forgive,
I won't forgive."

You Are Here

When I was in high school
I'd draw on all my shoes.

I'd cover my soles in
City skylines,
Song lyrics,
And Doctor Who quotes.

I scribbled on my pair of black converse
Block sharpie letters spelling

"You Are Here."

As a reminder,
That I am my own compass.

That the only way to live
Is to break my survival state
Into tiny little pieces,

To go back to the drawing board,
To create something new

To rebuild my world,
On what I know,
On what's real.

To show my brain
I can survive being here,
Being present.

That I don't need
Fantasies or illusions,
Just the ground beneath my feet.

No More Saviors

Why reinvent the wheel,
When the status quo already
Trickles down into their wallets?

When they can have their cake and eat it too.

At their corporate photo-ops for
Activism built on appearances
And feel good "acts of kindness."

It's all just pushing rocks up a hill,
A hill they never bother to dismantle,

Because they'd lose out on the praise
For all their hard work.

They pat themselves on the back,
Go back home,
Leave a couple of bills

And forget all about the people
At the bottom of the hill.

Mexico City

When I say
My family is from Mexico City

I'm talking about
Cempasuchil flowers
Covering Paseo De La Reforma.

The churro carts in Coyoacan.
And the boats in Xochimilco.

I'm talking about waking
Up to the sound of roosters,
And vendedores selling tamales y flanes.

I'm talking about trips to
The panaderia,
Y la papeleria,
Y la tortilleria.

Is it possible write about a city
Without romanticizing it?

Without mentioning the
Cinnamon sugar of pan dulce,
And the mariachi singing late into the night.

Without forgetting,

The pyramids
Waiting to rise up
From the Palacio Nacional
Or the students who never came home?

Ignoring the city's history

Taking pictures,
For the tourist guide
Explanation,

That glances over genocide
And slavery and ethnic cleansing.

Over green bandanas,
And riot shields
In front of El Zocalo.

Over Feminista y Zapatista
Slogans covering every wall

Otro Mundo Es Posible
No Estamos Solas
Ni Una Menos

I want to love the city that made me
Celebrate their resistance to neoliberal control,
Cry when their feminist president tugs on my heart strings.

But it feels like I'd be ignoring too much,
To wave a flag in the air,

I mean it can't be that different from any other state,
Any other government with the power to move mountains
Except when it matters.

Even if their faces look like mine,
And we had the same thing for breakfast,
Chilaquiles con frijoles y arroz y tostones.

Mexico city, a reminder,
That I got here on a coin toss,

That I could have easily been born
On the wrong side of the world.

This city is a reminder
To choose solidarity, to resist,

Racist, sexist, colorist norms
Used to oppress my people, my community.

Immigrant Moms

Immigrant moms taught me
The value of community,
They opened their homes,
They took care of me when my parents were away,

They fed me ice cream,
Drove me to school,
And fixed my glasses when they fell apart,

These moms taught me about mutual aid,

My parents always
Ensured that they were re-paid,

But I knew that's not why they helped,
They did it because they cared,

Because they weren't raised in cultures
That taught them to care only for themselves.

They were PTA moms,
Moms that brought their kids warm lunches to school,
Moms that painted henna on my hands during cultural days,
Moms who watched foreign dramas and *The View* with me

Moms who always brushed off their efforts,

*"Oh, it's no problem,
We had fun, didn't we?"*

They never saw themselves as revolutionary,
They didn't think of themselves as heroes,

Still, they made a difference in my life,

They showed me that another world was possible.

Honeybee

I got attached to a gummy worm
Someone dropped in the hallway
Outside my dorm room

It stayed there for days,
Gathering dust on the floor.

But I liked knowing it was there,
That it would greet me
On my way out the door.

I almost cried when
They vacuumed the hall,

Knowing my sugary friend,
Wouldn't be there to greet me
On my way to dinner.

Today, I tried to save a bee
Because it reminded me

Of the two little bees,
Walking in slow circles

On the floor of
My mother's classroom,
When I was a child.

Hypnotized by
Their quiet rhythm,
Their perfect orbit
I watched them dance.

Until,

One of my mom's students
Walked by and triumphantly
Crushed them under his boot.

One after the other.
I felt sad the whole way home.

So, today when I saw the bee,
Spinning around on the floor,

I reached out with a piece of paper
And carried him to a lemon tree full of flowers,

Where he could drink nectar,
Find other bees,

And stay hidden, stay safe
From vacuums, and men wearing boots.

Circus Lion

No one that loves you,
Seeks to control you

Or confine you,
In a shiny cage.

Watching as you put on a show
Licking your wounds and turning
Into a version of yourself
They can mold.

But no part of you is undeserving,
No part of you needs punishing.

And a cage is only a cage
When it is self-imposed.

You know,
Forgiveness isn't always revolutionary,
You don't have to be the guiding star

Just because you believe
The world can be good
Does not mean

You should squeeze
Every last drop of light
Out of the darkest places,

Out of people that dim your spark,
Suppress your light
And blame you for daring to shine.

You're always lighting the way,
Waiting for others to catch up.

But you're a luminary,
A warm beam of energy,
You were meant to be extraordinary.

It was never your burden to carry,
And it's not your fault,
If they can't match your flame.

Sometimes rage is the deepest form
Of love and care for yourself,
For your community.

It's time to
Light your own path,
Forge your own way.

And know that your presence
Will illuminate the lives,
Of those who choose to stay.

Love Poem: Sandcastle

My dad used to sing me a lullaby
About a house built on sand.

I'd fall asleep wondering if it was
A story about having faith in god
Or a story about making the right decisions.

Was it a story about discernment?
Or a warning
To beware big bad wolves
Looking to destroy houses
Made of straw and sand.

Or a lesson that even a strong house
Built with care and precision
Will fall if it's built in the wrong place.

I'd wake up in my crumbling sandcastle
Of a nervous system wondering why
I kept sinking into old cycles,

Never building anything long lasting,
Never finding anything fulfilling.

It's like my insides
Were full of seashells and sand,
Just a stack of traumas in a trench coat
My crab shell exterior just a front
For the scared sea foam girl hiding underneath.

This Time Around

"Don't lose that anger. Just have a little more patience and forgiveness. For yourself as well." - Larry Kramer, The Normal Heart

There's still a strong-willed child in me
Who doesn't want to let go of anything

She holds onto pain and grief,
Like some kind of emotional hoarder,
Never throwing anything away.

Time stopped when I was ten,
I had one foot in the past,
And one in the present.

Managing all the pain
I couldn't acknowledge, couldn't feel
Until I couldn't hold anymore,

Until my rage burned through all the pain,
All the shame that wasn't real.

Now times runs like sand
through an hourglass
It flows,
It flows,
It flows.

Love Poem: Obsidian

I resent the idea
That anger is a secondary emotion.
When it's the fuel that drives me,
The blood in my veins.

The rock that I stand on,
The values that ground me,
The light that shines through
Everything shattered part of me.

So, I'm sorry if I come off a bit hardheaded,
But I refuse to continue chipping
my rock into tiny pieces,

Because I never signed up to be your emotional punching
bag,
Someone to feel sorry for
Because I don't match up to the idea in your head.

When really, I am an island you'll never find the map to
return to.
A shore you'll never touch again.

So, fill your cup with rum,
Get behind the wheel,
And forget you ever knew me.

Artist

Sometimes, I wish
I was a better artist.

So, I could capture exactly
What I want to express,
Exactly how I feel.

A bird in a windstorm,
A worm with nowhere to hide.

I heard somewhere,
That we start healing
By telling the truth.

But what if I've been
Lying to myself so much
I can't remember what
What's real anymore?

Is it denial
Or survival?

And what if my anger is an arrow?
What if I just have to learn
To aim in the right direction?

What if my anger is just fuel?
Teaching me what to accept,
And what to reject,

Trying to show me
What to fight against.

What if I'm
Still learning to make an art
Of starting over?

An art
Of learning
And unlearning.

I Am My Own Archive

A catalog of everyone
I've ever been,

Everyone I've ever met
Is stored in the tissue
Of my nervous system,

Like I've stored the artifacts
From my childhood.

My old notebooks and CDs are
Packed away in boxes,
But the lyrics live in me.

Maybe love is a way
Of preserving,

Of passing down the story
Of who we are,

An archive enduring,
It's pages yellowing,
It's hearts unfolding,

Passing down the tale
Of history,
Of time.

Love Poem: Guinea Pig

Fuzzy noses,
And echoing squeals,

I clean their ears,
Provide all their meals.

They're loved and cared for,
Just for existing.

They sleep on
Soft pillows,
Get plenty of hay.

And greet me
In the morning
As I start the day.

They look up at me
With beady, innocent eyes,

Almost like they're
Waiting for me to realize,
Waiting for me to learn,

"Love isn't something you need to earn."

Happy Ending

My body is
Split in two.

From trying to stay in
A box that never fit me,
That was never made for me.

From trying to be nice
To my oppressors.

From trying to turn a cage,
Into a pillow fort sanctuary.

And dulling my teeth
To stay in places
Full of nails,
And knives.

From putting up blindfolds
To protect my eyes.

From trying to prove,
I could be more than a wound.

From pretending everyone
Knows better than me.

From tip toeing round their egos,
Just to keep them near me.

I read all these books
Just to push them aside,

The moment someone
Tells me they'd
be a better guide,

The chains are different now,
They're of my own making,

But I can create a new path,
Envision a better world,
A happier ending.

A world where I'm not
Ducking from arrows,
Or fighting dragons.

A world where
There are no walls to fall down,
No towers to escape from.

No soups,
That are too hot,
Or too cold.

I want a life
That's as real
As the salt in the sea

Golden like
The California coastline,
All sunshine and chaparral.

<u>Sisters</u>

*"The women were brave and beautiful their entire lives." - Shelley
Wong*

I didn't realize
I still believed in heaven

Until I was holding
My childhood best friend's hand

In the hospital
Minutes after she'd passed away.

Her sister standing over her,
Reminding us she wasn't alone,

All her ancestors were with her,
And all the friends
We'd said goodbye to years earlier.

I swear I could feel that she was there with us,
I mean, where else would she be

Then in a room with everyone
That loved her most?

She wasn't alone when she was here,
And she wasn't alone now.

Standing in that room,
Holding my best friends,

Twin sisters
Born minutes apart.

Like we were still 12 years old,
Unaware that anything bad could ever happen.
Or that we would ever be apart.

New Year's Eve in Joshua Tree

"You really want to go to the desert,
With a bunch of gay people?

I mean, what do you expect to happen?"

What I expect

I expect to feel free,
To feel safe,
Feel the sigh of relief

From being miles away from
People who question my every decision,

Who think my bids for connection,
        Are requests for permission

Then wonder why I end up with people
Who only want to control me.
        And never listen when I say "no."

But what do they expect?

I imagine our hands clasped in a circle; voices joined in unison:

"I swear to the Joshua Trees and the Salton Sea
To reject Jesus and watch Rupal religiously,
To give myself a weird haircut
And never step foot in a church again"

My parent's eyes are full of fear,
And suddenly I recognize their anxiety,

My fear has never been mine
It was inherited,

Born from sheltered Christians,
Who think everything is a slippery slope into sin.

You know, for people
That preach abstinence,

Christians are weirdly preoccupied
With sex, imagining all the scary
Scenarios their children could find themselves in.

What really happens in Joshua Tree

We watch Rupal lip sync battles,
Play charades, and eat ice cream in our PJs

We eat grapes under the table at midnight

We drive through the desert
To see the stars.

We spot constellations
Like amateur astronomers.

We rest on hammocks in the backyard
Feeling the chill in the air.

We sit and watch headlights reflect off yucca trees.
Trying to keep our hands warm
By shoving them into our pockets.

We laugh and take blurry photos of each other,

The flash illuminating
Our faces before going dark.

Orion's Belt

I used to get sad in the winter,
It's as if my life would stop
When the sun would set.

The cold would stay in my
Hands and slip through my socks.
A chill I couldn't escape.

When you were near me,
It's like all the light
Turned into shadows.

I'd come find you in the forest,
Down the barely lit path you'd chosen.
You'd point up at the stars
And name them,

While I'd cling to your arm,
Trying to stay warm.

It took me months to fix
My appetite,

I survived off chicken noodle soup,
And air-fried potatoes

Until I couldn't see my chilled breath
In the air anymore.

Now the sun lives in me,
Shining through warm brown eyes,
And the frozen tree skyline.

Thawing all the winter snow,
Into melted sunshine.

We Were Girls Together

The pastor gets on the pulpit and says,
"We're all going to die someday."

That Jesus died for your sins,
So, it's okay to be sad,
But you're in a better place.

You know, I've never thought much of pastors,
I've scorned them my whole life,

And I think it should be illegal
To call someone a sinner
At their funeral,

She was my best friend,
My honorary sister,
Her sins are my sins,

"Can you hear this, Shelly?"

Can you hear your twin sister give a eulogy,
About all you've endured?

Can you hear us laughing about
All the happiness you brought us,
And all the memories we get to keep?

I look up at pictures of you
Surrounded by flowers and loved ones thinking,

If your life was worth remembering,
If your life impacted me and everyone in this room,

Then maybe my life is meaningful too,
Not because of my degrees,
Or the status I've worked so hard to achieve,

But because of the friends I made when I was 17.

She Visits Me in Dreams

She wears her red AYSO uniform
She rests her head on my shoulder,
She tells me about a new boy she's seeing,
She brushes her hair behind her ear,
She shows me her new press-on nails.

She talks to her sister,
And she dances,
Like she never left,

Like I could just drive to her apartment,
And find her sitting on the front steps.

Love Poem: Lantern

I keep forgetting to tell you,
I'm playing a game that reminds me of you.

I keep forgetting to tell you,
I'm playing a song that reminds me of you.

I keep forgetting to tell you,
that you're the light at the end of this tunnel.

You drew the map, and now I know the way.

Acknowledgments

Thank you to Ceasar K. Avelar my poetry teacher and mentor, who was always there at the end of my open mics with a "That was fire!" Thank you so much for welcoming into the Pomona poetry scene!

Erica my wonderful publisher! Thanks for your support and the opportunity to publish my work!

My lovely poetry friends Alondra Dara, Ruby Ramos, Sammy Herrera, and Consuelo, thank you for reading my work and being there for me! You are all so talented! Check out all their upcoming books and open mic performances!

Thank you to my mentors and professors, Dr. Anthony Bernier and Dr. Mike Males, for teaching me so much about research, youth rights, and helping me think critically about everything!

Thank you to everyone who I worked with at Library Futures, Michelle Reed, Jennie Rose Halpern, and Laura Crossett! I learned so much from my internship and appreciate all your support!

To my sister Damaris and her boyfriend, Steven Jimenez, for supporting me and encouraging me to publish my work! To my parents and family for your support!

To Sanai West and her family! Thank you, Sanai, for always being a friend I can rely on and reminding me what emotional safety feels like. All my best memories are with you too! Thank you to the West family for taking me on adventures and letting me spend so much time at your houses! To Emma Dawsey, thank you for always reaching out and being a friend when I needed one! Thanks for getting me into scary movies and always sharing your media recommendations with me!

Frances Catalan, Litzia Itzel, Dylan Reinders and Edward Estrada. I'm so glad I signed up to live on the queer floor of Porter because I got to meet all of you!

To the feminists on social media who saved my life, Cecilia Regina and Melanie Hamlett.

I also wrote several of these poems in a workshop led by Ariana Brown, and Alan Peleaz Lopez, where we used ghost lines from other poems, so here are the credits!

Citrus Roots was inspired by Eve Ewing's poem *I come from the fire city* from Eve Ewing's poetry collection *1919*. It was also originally published in the ILL Anthology

Donika Kelly's poetry collection Bestiary inspired the Love Poem series

The lines "think of the body as" and "I know you are familiar with" from *Love Poem: Puddle* are ghost lines from *am-phib-ian* by Jessica Lanay

Disguise / Desire borrows "without epiphany or struggle" from -*Alex Dimitrov's love and other poems; "suddenly summer."*

Seeking A Born Collaborator was originally published in the 8th issue of Wizards in Space Literary Magazine.

Author Bio

Milo Santamaria (she / they) is a queer Latinx poet from Southern California. Milo is a feminist abolitionist, and their work focuses on ending cycles of violence and abuse. With a bachelor's degree in sociology from UC Santa Cruz, and a master's degree in library science from San Jose State, they bring a deep understanding of societal structures to their writing, crafting work that is both personal and political. Their poems have been included in zines and publications such as Wizards in Space Literary Magazine, Queering Friendships Zine and the ILL Poetry Anthology. They have also written articles and blog posts for Library Futures and Youth Facts, a blog centered on youth rights and activism.

You can find Milo on Instagram @milo_s64, and @glittertimes on Tumblr!

Publishers Note

Daxson publishing was created to help marginalized artists and their allies publish their work, so the world can hear their voice. The vision for this publishing house is to help people get their work out there, and not have them struggle finding their way through the publishing process. Everyone's voice deserves to be heard, and we are here to help. If you are interested in submitting a manuscript, email daxsonpublishing@gmail.com. Purchase our books at daxsonpublishing.com